MERCIAN HYMNS

*

GEOFFREY HILL

*

ANDRE DEUTSCH

First published 1971 by
André Deutsch Limited
105 Great Russell Street, London WC1

Printed in Great Britain by
Clarke Doble & Brendon Ltd, Plymouth

ISBN 0 233 95770 7 (casebound)
ISBN 0 233 95771 5 (paperback)

821

H1L

MERCIAN HYMNS

By the same author

FOR THE UNFALLEN

KING LOG

The conduct of government rests upon the same foundation and encounters the same difficulties as the conduct of private persons: that is, as to its object and justification, for as to its methods, or technical part, there is all the difference which separates the person from the group, the man acting on behalf of himself from the man acting on behalf of many. The technical part, in government as in private conduct, is now the only one which is publicly or at any rate generally recognised, as if by this evasion the more difficult part of the subject, which relates to ends, could be avoided. Upon 'the law of nature and the law of revelation', Blackstone said, 'depend all human laws.' This quaint language, which would at once be derided if it were introduced now into public discussion, conceals a difficulty which is no less ours than it was our ancestors'.

C. H. SISSON

I

King of the perennial holly-groves, the riven sand-
stone: overlord of the M5: architect of the his-
toric rampart and ditch, the citadel at Tamworth,
the summer hermitage in Holy Cross: guardian of
the Welsh Bridge and the Iron Bridge: contractor
to the desirable new estates: saltmaster: money-
changer: commissioner for oaths: martyrologist:
the friend of Charlemagne.

'I liked that,' said Offa, 'sing it again.'

II

A pet-name, a common name. Best-selling brand, curt
    graffito. A laugh; a cough. A syndicate. A specious
    gift. Scoffed-at horned phonograph.

The starting-cry of a race. A name to conjure with.

III

On the morning of the crowning we chorused our re-
mission from school. It was like Easter: hankies
and gift-mugs approved by his foreign gaze, the
village-lintels curlered with paper flags.

We gaped at the car-park of 'The Stag's Head' where a
bonfire of beer-crates and holly-boughs whistled
above the tar. And the chef stood there, a king in
his new-risen hat, sealing his brisk largesse with
'any mustard?'

IV

I was invested in mother-earth, the crypt of roots
  and endings. Child's-play. I abode there, bided my
  time: where the mole

shouldered the clogged wheel, his gold solidus; where
  dry-dust badgers thronged the Roman flues, the
  long-unlooked-for mansions of our tribe.

V

So much for the elves' wergild, the true governance
of England, the gaunt warrior-gospel armoured in
engraved stone. I wormed my way heavenward for
ages amid barbaric ivy, scrollwork of fern.

Exile or pilgrim set me once more upon that ground:
my rich and desolate childhood. Dreamy, smug-faced,
sick on outings—I who was taken to be a king of
some kind, a prodigy, a maimed one.

VI

The princes of Mercia were badger and raven. Thrall
to their freedom, I dug and hoarded. Orchards
fruited above clefts. I drank from honeycombs of
chill sandstone.

'A boy at odds in the house, lonely among brothers.'
But I, who had none, fostered a strangeness; gave
myself to unattainable toys.

Candles of gnarled resin, apple-branches, the tacky
mistletoe. 'Look' they said and again 'look.' But
I ran slowly; the landscape flowed away, back to
its source.

In the schoolyard, in the cloakrooms, the children
boasted their scars of dried snot; wrists and
knees garnished with impetigo.

VII

Gasholders, russet among fields. Milldams, marlpools
that lay unstirring. Eel-swarms. Coagulations of
frogs: once, with branches and half-bricks, he
battered a ditchful; then sidled away from the
stillness and silence.

Ceolred was his friend and remained so, even after
the day of the lost fighter: a biplane, already
obsolete and irreplaceable, two inches of heavy
snub silver. Ceolred let it spin through a hole
in the classroom-floorboards, softly, into the
rat-droppings and coins.

After school he lured Ceolred, who was sniggering
with fright, down to the old quarries, and flayed
him. Then, leaving Ceolred, he journeyed for hours,
calm and alone, in his private derelict sandlorry
named *Albion*.

VIII

The mad are predators. Too often lately they harbour
  against us. A novel heresy exculpates all maimed
  souls. Abjure it! I am the King of Mercia, and
  I know.

Threatened by phone-calls at midnight, venomous let-
  ters, forewarned I have thwarted their imminent
  devices.

Today I name them; tomorrow I shall express the new
  law. I dedicate my awakening to this matter.

IX

The strange church smelled a bit 'high', of censers
and polish. The strange curate was just as ap-
propriate: he took off into the marriage-service.
No-one cared to challenge that gambit.

Then he dismissed you, and the rest of us followed,
sheepish next-of-kin, to the place without the
walls: spoil-heaps of chrysanths dead in their
plastic macs, eldorado of washstand-marble.

Embarrassed, we dismissed ourselves: the three mute
great-aunts borne away down St Chad's Garth in
a stiff-backed Edwardian Rolls.

I unburden the saga of your burial, my dear. You had
lived long enough to see things 'nicely settled'.

B

X

He adored the desk, its brown-oak inlaid with ebony,
assorted prize pens, the seals of gold and base
metal into which he had sunk his name.

It was there that he drew upon grievances from the
people; attended to signatures and retributions;
forgave the death-howls of his rival. And there
he exchanged gifts with the Muse of History.

What should a man make of remorse, that it might
profit his soul? Tell me. Tell everything to
Mother, darling, and God bless.

He swayed in sunlight, in mild dreams. He tested the
little pears. He smeared catmint on his palm for
his cat Smut to lick. He wept, attempting to mas-
ter *ancilla* and *servus*.

XI

Coins handsome as Nero's; of good substance and weight. *Offa Rex* resonant in silver, and the names of his moneyers. They struck with accountable tact. They could alter the king's face.

Exactness of design was to deter imitation; mutilation if that failed. Exemplary metal, ripe for commerce. Value from a sparse people, scrapers of salt-pans and byres.

Swathed bodies in the long ditch; one eye upstaring. It is safe to presume, here, the king's anger. He reigned forty years. Seasons touched and retouched the soil.

Heathland, new-made watermeadow. Charlock, marshmarigold. Crepitant oak forest where the boar furrowed black mould, his snout intimate with worms and leaves.

XII

Their spades grafted through the variably-resistant
soil. They clove to the hoard. They ransacked epi-
phanies, vertebrae of the chimera, armour of wild
bees' larvae. They struck the fire-dragon's fac-
eted skin.

The men were paid to caulk water-pipes. They brewed
and pissed amid splendour; their latrine seethed
its estuary through nettles. They are scattered
to your collations, moldywarp.

It is autumn. Chestnut-boughs clash their inflamed
leaves. The garden festers for attention: telluric
cultures enriched with shards, corms, nodules, the
sunk solids of gravity. I have accrued a golden
and stinking blaze.

XIII

Trim the lamp; polish the lens; draw, one by one, rare
coins to the light. Ringed by its own lustre, the
masterful head emerges, kempt and jutting, out of
England's well. Far from his underkingdom of crin-
oid and crayfish, the rune-stone's province, *Rex
Totius Anglorum Patriae*, coiffured and ageless,
portrays the self-possession of his possession,
cushioned on a legend.

XIV

Dismissing reports and men, he put pressure on the wax, blistered it to a crest. He threatened malefactors with ash from his noon cigar.

When the sky cleared above Malvern, he lingered in his orchard; by the quiet hammer-pond. Trout-fry simmered there, translucent, as though forming the water's underskin. He had a care for natural minutiae. What his gaze touched was his tenderness. Woodlice sat pellet-like in the cracked bark and a snail sugared its new stone.

At dinner, he relished the mockery of drinking his family's health. He did this whenever it suited him, which was not often.

XV

Tutting, he wrenched at a snarled root of dead crab-
apple. It rose against him. In brief cavort he was
Cernunnos, the branched god, lightly concussed.

He divided his realm. It lay there like a dream. An
ancient land, full of strategy. Ramparts of com-
post pioneered by red-helmeted worms. Hemlock in
ambush, night-soil, tetanus. A wasps' nest en-
sconced in the hedge-bank, a reliquary or wrapped
head, the corpse of Cernunnos pitching dayward
its feral horns.

XVI

Clash of salutation. As keels thrust into shingle.
Ambassadors, pilgrims. What is carried over? The
Frankish gift, two-edged, regaled with slaughter.

The sword is in the king's hands; the crux a crafts-
man's triumph. Metal effusing its own fragrance,
a variety of balm. And other miracles, other
exchanges.

Shafts from the winter sun homing upon earth's rim.
Christ's mass: in the thick of a snowy forest the
flickering evergreen fissured with light.

Attributes assumed, retribution entertained. What is
borne amongst them? Too much or too little. In-
dulgences of bartered acclaim; an expenditure, a
hissing. Wine, urine and ashes.

XVII

He drove at evening through the hushed Vosges. The
car radio, glimmering, received broken utterance
from the horizon of storms . . .

'God's honour—our bikes touched; he skidded and came
off.' 'Liar.' A timid father's protective bellow.
Disfigurement of a village-king. 'Just look at
the bugger . . .'

His maroon GT chanted then overtook. He lavished on
the high valleys its *haleine*.

XVIII

At Pavia, a visitation of some sorrow. Boethius'
dungeon. He shut his eyes, gave rise to a tower
out of the earth. He willed the instruments of
violence to break upon meditation. Iron buckles
gagged; flesh leaked rennet over them; the men
stooped, disentangled the body.

He wiped his lips and hands. He strolled back to the
car, with discreet souvenirs for consolation and
philosophy. He set in motion the furtherance of
his journey. To watch the Tiber foaming out
much blood.

XIX

Behind the thorn-trees thin smoke, scutch-grass or
wattle smouldering. At this distance it is hard
to tell. Far cries impinge like the faint tink-
ing of iron.

We have a kitchen-garden riddled with toy-shards,
with splinters of habitation. The children shriek
and scavenge, play havoc. They incinerate boxes,
rags and old tyres. They haul a sodden log, hung
with soft shields of fungus, and launch it upon
the flames.

XX

Primeval heathland spattered with the bones of mice
and birds; where adders basked and bees made pro-
vision, mantling the inner walls of their burh :

Coiled entrenched England : brickwork and paintwork
stalwart above hacked marl. The clashing prim-
ary colours—'Ethandune', 'Catraeth', 'Maldon',
'Pengwern'. Steel against yew and privet. Fresh
dynasties of smiths.

XXI

Cohorts of charabancs fanfared Offa's province and
his concern, negotiating the by-ways from Teme
to Trent. Their windshields dripped butterflies.
Stranded on hilltops they signalled with plumes
of steam. Twilight menaced the land. The young
women wept and surrendered.

Still, everyone was cheerful, heedless in such days:
at summer weekends dipping into valleys beyond
Mercia's dyke. Tea was enjoyed, by lakesides where
all might fancy carillons of real Camelot vib-
rating through the silent water.

Gradually, during the years, deciduous velvet peeled
from evergreen albums and during the years more
treasures were mislaid: the harp-shaped brooches,
the nuggets of fool's gold.

XXII

We ran across the meadow scabbed with cow-dung, past
   the crab-apple trees and camouflaged nissen hut.
   It was curfew-time for our war-band.

At home the curtains were drawn. The wireless boomed
   its commands. I loved the battle-anthems and the
   gregarious news.

Then, in the earthy shelter, warmed by a blue-glassed
   storm-lantern, I huddled with stories of dragon-
   tailed airships and warriors who took wing im-
   mortal as phantoms.

XXIII

In tapestries, in dreams, they gathered, as it was en-
acted, the return, the re-entry of transcendence
into this sublunary world. *Opus Anglicanum,* their
stringent mystery riddled by needles: the silver
veining, the gold leaf, voluted grape-vine, master-
works of treacherous thread.

They trudged out of the dark, scraping their boots
free from lime-splodges and phlegm. They munched
cold bacon. The lamps grew plump with oily re-
liable light.

XXIV

Itinerant through numerous domains, of his lord's
 retinue, to Compostela. Then home for a lifetime
 amid West Mercia this master-mason as I envisage
 him, intent to pester upon tympanum and chancel-
 arch his moody testament, confusing warrior with
 lion, dragon-coils, tendrils of the stony vine.

Where best to stand? Easter sunrays catch the ob-
 lique face of Adam scrumping through leaves; pale
 spree of evangelists and, there, a cross Christ
 mumming child Adam out of Hell

('Et exspecto resurrectionem mortuorum' dust in the
 eyes, on clawing wings, and lips)

XXV

Brooding on the eightieth letter of *Fors Clavigera*,
I speak this in memory of my grandmother, whose
childhood and prime womanhood were spent in the
nailer's darg.

The nailshop stood back of the cottage, by the fold.
It reeked stale mineral sweat. Sparks had furred
its low roof. In dawn-light the troughed water
floated a damson-bloom of dust—

not to be shaken by posthumous clamour. It is one
thing to celebrate the 'quick forge', another
to cradle a face hare-lipped by the searing wire.

Brooding on the eightieth letter of *Fors Clavigera*,
I speak this in memory of my grandmother, whose
childhood and prime womanhood were spent in the
nailer's darg.

XXVI

Fortified in their front parlours, at Yuletide men
are the more murderous. Drunk, they defy battle-
axes, bellow of whale-bone and dung.

Troll-wives, groaners in sweetness, tooth-bewitchers,
you too must purge for the surfeit of England—
who have scattered peppermint and confetti, your
hundreds-and-thousands.

XXVII

'Now when King Offa was alive and dead', they were all there, the funereal gleemen: papal legate and rural dean; Merovingian car-dealers, Welsh mercenaries; a shuffle of house-carls.

He was defunct. They were perfunctory. The ceremony stood acclaimed. The mob received memorial vouchers and signs.

After that shadowy, thrashing midsummer hail-storm, Earth lay for a while, the ghost-bride of livid Thor, butcher of strawberries, and the shire-tree dripped red in the arena of its uprooting.

XXVIII

Processes of generation; deeds of settlement. The urge to marry well; wit to invest in the properties of healing-springs. Our children and our children's children, o my masters.

Tracks of ancient occupation. Frail ironworks rusting in the thorn-thicket. Hearthstones; charred lullabies. A solitary axe-blow that is the echo of a lost sound.

Tumult recedes as though into the long rain. Groves of legendary holly; silverdark the ridged gleam.

XXIX

'Not strangeness, but strange likeness. Obstinate, outclassed forefathers, I too concede, I am your staggeringly-gifted child.'

So, murmurous, he withdrew from them. Gran lit the gas, his dice whirred in the ludo-cup, he entered into the last dream of Offa the King.

XXX

And it seemed, while we waited, he began to walk to-
wards us   he vanished

he left behind coins, for his lodging, and traces of
red mud.

❀

LIST OF HYMNS

ACKNOWLEDGMENTS

The historical King Offa reigned over Mercia (and the greater part of England south of the Humber) in the years AD 757–796. During early medieval times he was already becoming a creature of legend. The Offa who figures in this sequence might perhaps most usefully be regarded as the presiding genius of the West Midlands, his dominion enduring from the middle of the eighth century until the middle of the twentieth (and possibly beyond). The indication of such a timespan will, I trust, explain and to some extent justify a number of anachronisms.

I have a duty to acknowledge that the authorities cited in these notes might properly object to their names being used in so unscholarly and fantastic a context. I have no wish to compromise the accurate scholarship of others. Having taken over certain statements and references from my reading and having made them a part of the idiom of this sequence, I believe that I should acknowledge the sources. I have specified those debts of which I am aware. Possibly there are others of which I am unaware. If that is so I regret the oversight.

The title of the sequence is a suggestion taken from

Sweet's Anglo-Saxon Reader, Oxford (Twelfth Edition, 1950), pp. 170–80. A less-immediate precedent is provided by the Latin prose-hymns or canticles of the early Christian Church. See Frederick Brittain, ed., *The Penguin Book of Latin Verse*, Harmondsworth (1962), pp. xvii, lv.

II: 'a common name' cf. W. F. Bolton, *A History of Anglo-Latin Literature 597–1066*, Princeton (1967), I, p. 191 : 'But Offa is a common name'.

IV : 'I was invested in mother-earth'. To the best of my recollection, the expression 'to invest in mother-earth' was the felicitous (and correct) definition of 'yird' given by Mr Michael Hordern in the programme *Call My Bluff* televised on BBC 2 on Thursday January 29th 1970.

V : 'wergild' : 'the price set upon a man according to his rank' (O.E.D.) cf. D. Whitelock, *The Beginnings of English Society*, Harmondsworth (1965 edition), ch. 5.

XI: 'Offa Rex': an inscription on his coins. See J. J. North, *English Hammered Coinage*, London (1963), I, pp. 52–60 and Plate III.

XIII : 'Rex Totius Anglorum Patriae': 'King of the Whole Country of the English'. See Christopher Brooke, *The Saxon and Norman Kings*, London (1967 edition), p. 200.

XV : 'Cernunnos' : cf. *Larousse Encyclopedia of Mythology*, London (1960 edition), pp. 235, 244, 246–8.

XVII: 'haleine': cf. *La Chanson de Roland*, ed.

F. Whitehead, Oxford (1942), 1789, 'Ço dist li reis: "Cel corn ad lunge aleine." '

XVIII : 'for consolation and philosophy' : the allusion is to the title of Boethius' great meditation, though it is doubtless an excess of scruple to point this out.

'To watch the Tiber foaming out much blood' : adapted from Vergil, *Aeneid*, VI, 87, 'et Thybrim multo spumantem sanguine cerno'.

XX : 'Ethandune', 'Catraeth', 'Maldon', 'Pengwern' : in this context supposedly the names of English suburban dwellings. Ethandune = the Battle of Edington (Wilts), AD 878; Catraeth = the Battle of Catterick, late sixth century; Maldon = the Battle of Maldon, AD 991; Pengwern (Shrewsbury), capital of the Princes of Powys, taken by Offa, AD 779. See Anthony Conran, ed., *The Penguin Book of Welsh Verse*, Harmondsworth (1967), pp. 24–30, 75–78, 90–93; Richard Hamer, ed., *A Choice of Anglo-Saxon Verse*, London (1970), pp. 48–69; A. H. Smith, ed., *The Parker Chronicle*, London (Third Edition, 1951), pp. 31–2.

XXIII : '*Opus Anglicanum*': the term is properly applicable to English embroidery of the period AD 1250–1350, though the craft was already famous some centuries earlier. See A. G. I. Christie, *English Medieval Embroidery*, Oxford (1938), pp. 1–2. In XXIV and XXV I have, with considerable impropriety, extended the term to apply to English Romanesque sculpture and to utilitarian metal-work of the nineteenth century.

XXIV: for the association of Compostela with West Midlands sculpture of the twelfth century I am indebted to G. Zarnecki, *Later English Romanesque Sculpture*, London (1953), esp. pp. 9–15, 'The Herefordshire School'.

'Et exspecto resurrectionem mortuorum': a debt to Olivier Messiaen, his music 'for orchestra of woodwind, brass and metallic percussion'.

XXV: 'the eightieth letter of *Fors Clavigera*'. See *The Works of John Ruskin*, London (1903–1912), XXIX, pp. 170–180.

'darg': 'a day's work, the task of a day . . .' (O.E.D.). Ruskin employs the word, here and elsewhere.

'quick forge': see W. Shakespeare, *Henry V*, V, Chorus, 23. The phrase requires acknowledgment but the source has no bearing on the poem.

'wire': I seem not to have been strictly accurate. Hand-made nails were forged from rods. Wire was used for the 'French nails' made by machine. But: 'wire' = 'metal wrought into the form of a slender rod or thread' (O.E.D.).

XXVII: 'Now when King Offa was alive and dead' is based on a ritual phrase used of various kings though not, as far as I am aware, of Offa himself. See Christopher Brooke, *op. cit*, p. 39; R. H. M. Dolley, ed., *Anglo-Saxon Coins: Studies Presented to F. M. Stenton*, London (1961), p. 220.